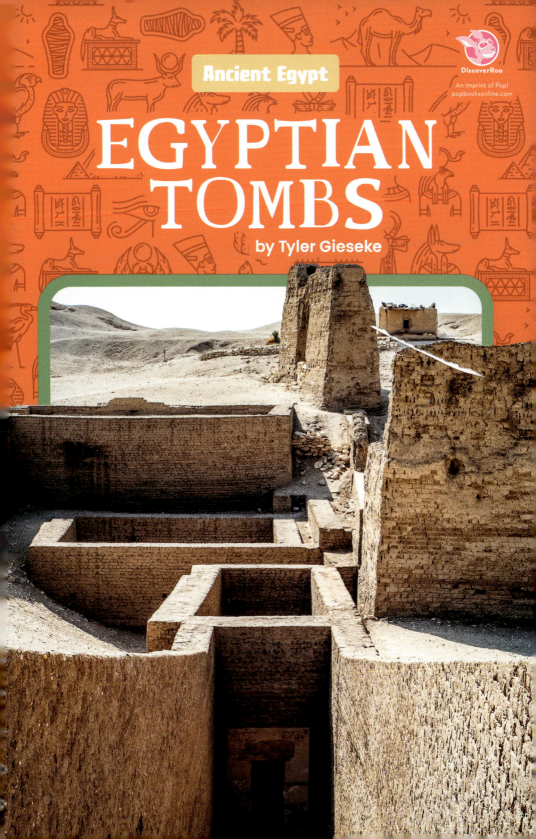

abdobooks.com

Published by Pop!, a division of ABDO, PO Box 398166, Minneapolis, Minnesota 55439. Copyright ©2022 by Abdo Consulting Group, Inc. International copyrights reserved in all countries. No part of this book may be reproduced in any form without written permission from the publisher. DiscoverRoo™ is a trademark and logo of Pop!.

Printed in the United States of America, North Mankato, Minnesota.

052021
092021

THIS BOOK CONTAINS RECYCLED MATERIALS

Cover Photos: Shutterstock Images
Interior Photos: Shutterstock Images, 1, 9, 13, 17, 21; bumihills/Shutterstock.com, 5; Vladimir Melnik/Shutterstock.com, 6; iStockphoto, 11, 14–15, 28, 29 (bottom); kritsadap/Shutterstock.com, 18–19; mountainpix/Shutterstock.com, 23; ichywong/Shutterstock.com, 24–25; Ivan Sebborn/Alamy, 26; Danita Delimont/Shutterstock.com, 29 (top)

Editor: Elizabeth Andrews
Series Designer: Laura Graphenteen

Library of Congress Control Number: 2020948835
Publisher's Cataloging-in-Publication Data
Names: Gieseke, Tyler, author.
Title: Egyptian tombs / by Tyler Gieseke
Description: Minneapolis, Minnesota : Pop!, 2022 | Series: Ancient Egypt | Includes online resources and index.
Identifiers: ISBN 9781532169885 (lib. bdg.) | ISBN 9781644945353 (pbk.) | ISBN 9781098240813 (ebook)
Subjects: LCSH: Tombs--Egypt--Juvenile literature. | Pyramids--Egypt--Juvenile literature. | Funeral rites and ceremonies--Egypt--Juvenile literature. | Egypt--History--Juvenile literature. | Afterlife--Juvenile literature.
Classification: DDC 932.01--dc23

WELCOME TO DiscoverRoo!

Pop open this book and you'll find QR codes loaded with information, so you can learn even more!

Scan this code* and others like it while you read, or visit the website below to make this book pop!

popbooksonline.com/egyptian-tombs

*Scanning QR codes requires a web-enabled smart device with a QR code reader app and a camera.

TABLE OF CONTENTS

CHAPTER 1
Honoring the Dead 4

CHAPTER 2
Mastabas and Pyramids. 10

CHAPTER 3
Valley of the Kings 16

CHAPTER 4
Famous Tombs 22

Making Connections. 30
Glossary 31
Index. 32
Online Resources 32

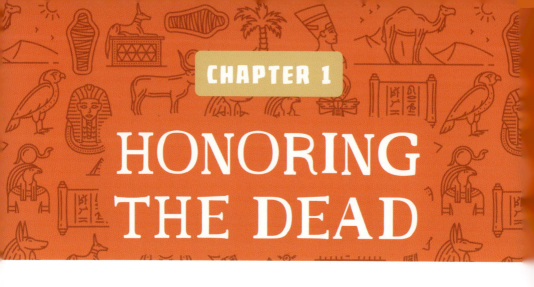

CHAPTER 1
HONORING THE DEAD

An **archaeologist** speaks to a worker at an Egyptian dig area. The desert winds can be forceful. The archaeologist has to raise her voice so the worker can hear her.

WATCH A VIDEO HERE!

Digging teams in Egypt search for ancient tombs and other treasures.

The walls of Egyptian tombs often have beautiful artwork and writing on them.

The archaeologist and her team are digging in the Valley of the Kings. There, scientists have found the tombs of

many ancient Egyptian rulers. Maybe the archaeologist's team will find another.

A tomb is a place where people bury or put their dead. The tomb is supposed to honor the life of the dead person.

Ancient Egyptian tombs have interested scientists, explorers, and even robbers for thousands of years. People can find treasures inside tombs. They can learn about how the dead person lived. And, they can learn about the people who created the tomb.

Tombs were very important in ancient Egypt. They were mainly for wealthy leaders. Egyptians believed that people who died could use the things in their tombs during the **afterlife**. So, wealthy people often kept their nicest things in their tombs.

Egyptian tombs took many forms. They could be simple stone rooms, deep

DID YOU KNOW? Some tombs had traps to stop robbers from stealing!

Piles of gold and other riches in Egyptian tombs made them targets for robbers.

caves, or towering **pyramids**! People can learn a lot about ancient Egypt by studying Egyptian tombs.

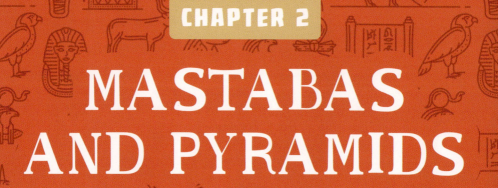

CHAPTER 2
MASTABAS AND PYRAMIDS

Ancient Egyptian society was around for about 3,000 years. Tombs from different time periods did not look alike. The tombs changed as the Egyptians' skills and styles changed.

LEARN MORE HERE!

Scientists believe this mastaba was for a top official. The pharaoh chose officials. They were highly respected.

Early Egyptian leaders built rectangular stone tombs with flat roofs. These were called *mastabas*. Mastabas were somewhat easy to build.

The **pharaoh** Djoser wanted more than a mastaba for his tomb. He had workers construct the Step **Pyramid**. It looked like several mastabas on top of each other.

Later pharaohs had workers make more pyramids. These pyramids were difficult to build. The pharaoh

> ### BUILDING A PYRAMID
>
> Building a pyramid was not as simple as constructing a mastaba. Scientists think farmers worked for months every year to build the Great Pyramid of Giza. It still took 20 years to build. Each stone weighed about 2.5 short tons (2.3 metric tons). And workers only had one day off every ten days!

Snefru directed people to build the first pyramid with smooth sides. This pyramid was not balanced. It almost fell down. It is called the Bent Pyramid.

The angle of the Bent Pyramid's walls changes in the middle.

Khufu was Snefru's son. As pharaoh, Khufu had laborers construct the largest pyramid yet. The Great Pyramid of Giza was about 480 feet (146 meters) tall. But people took the outer layer, made of polished white limestone. Today the Pyramid is 451 feet (137 meters) tall.

DID YOU KNOW? The Great Pyramid was the tallest structure in the world for at least 3,000 years.

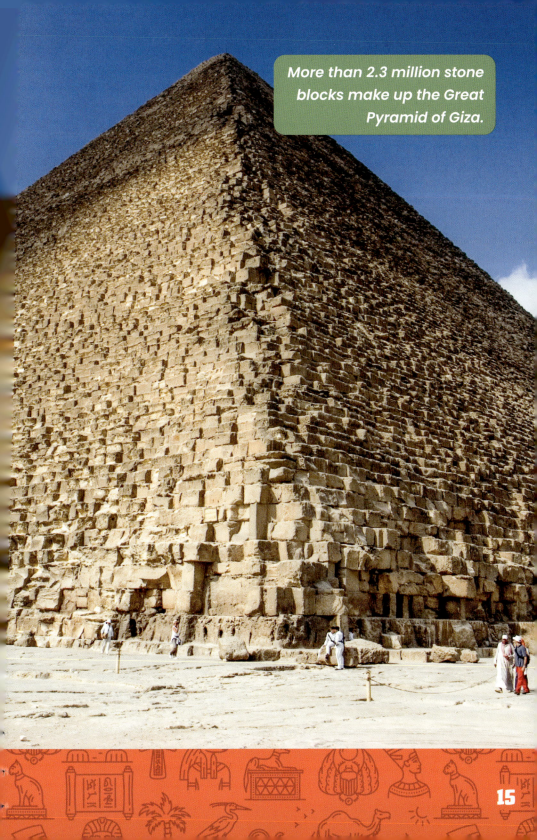

More than 2.3 million stone blocks make up the Great Pyramid of Giza.

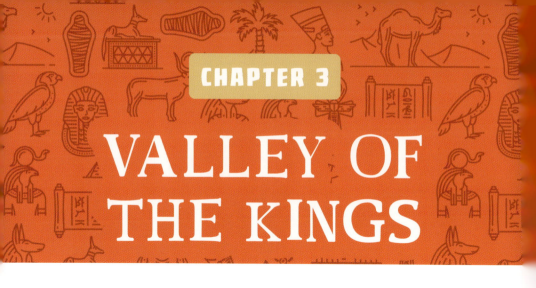

CHAPTER 3
VALLEY OF THE KINGS

As time went on, the ancient Egyptians didn't have enough resources to construct giant **pyramids**. Pyramids became smaller.

COMPLETE AN ACTIVITY HERE!

Tombs in the Valley of the Kings went deep into the ground.

Although they weren't tall like pyramids, cave tombs were still fancy.

Eventually, **pharaohs** stopped creating pyramids altogether. Pyramids were huge tasks. And, robbers often broke in and stole riches. Instead, pharaohs used caves for their tombs. These tombs were in a special place. It was called the Valley of the Kings.

DID YOU KNOW? Some tombs had *ushabti*, or small figures meant to come alive and work for the dead person in the **underworld**.

The pharaohs hoped these deep tombs would keep their things safe from robbers. Many rulers had their tombs sealed for safety. They also kept the locations secret.

Still, robbers were very smart. They began to find the tombs. In about 1000 BCE, priests moved royal **mummies** from the Valley of the Kings to other secret areas. Eventually, people found these mummies too. But it took almost 3,000 years!

INSIDE A TOMB

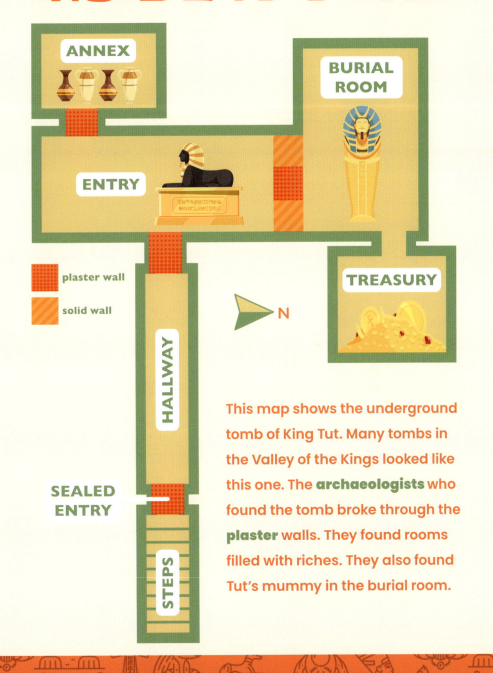

This map shows the underground tomb of King Tut. Many tombs in the Valley of the Kings looked like this one. The **archaeologists** who found the tomb broke through the **plaster** walls. They found rooms filled with riches. They also found Tut's mummy in the burial room.

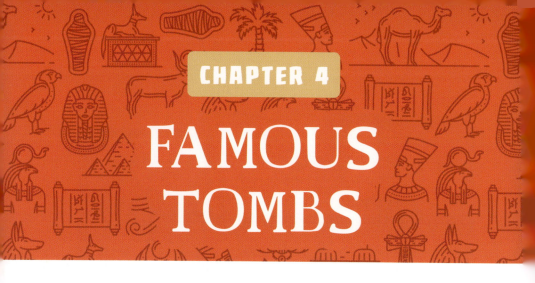

CHAPTER 4
FAMOUS TOMBS

Some tombs were so noticeable or held so much wealth that they are now famous. Many of these are open to tourists today.

LEARN MORE HERE!

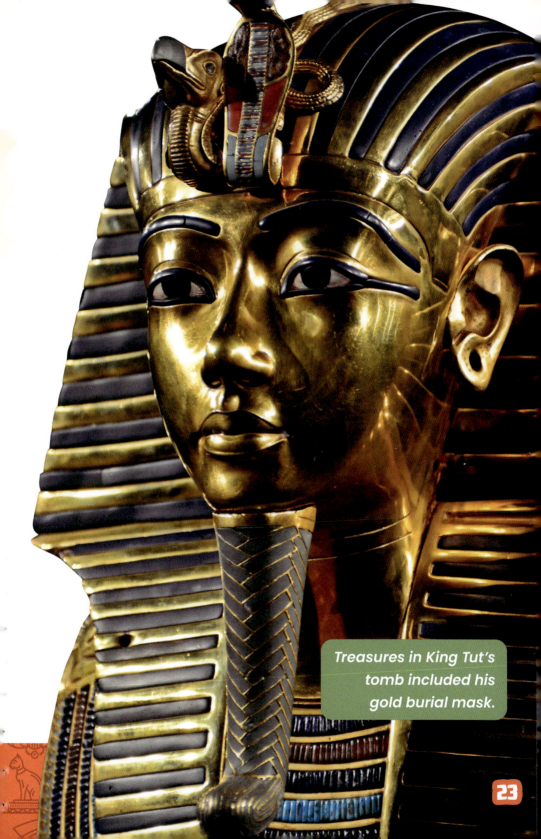

Treasures in King Tut's tomb included his gold burial mask.

The tomb of the **pharaoh** Tutankhamon, or King Tut, is in the Valley of the Kings. The **archaeologist** Howard Carter found it in 1922 CE. A royal seat was inside, along with vases, couches, and many other things.

DID YOU KNOW? It took more than ten years to take all the riches out of King Tut's tomb.

Visitors can see several mastabas near Saqqara, Egypt. Ancient Egyptians buried government and palace workers here. Djoser's Step **Pyramid** is also at Saqqara.

The Step Pyramid was one of the first Egyptian buildings made completely of stone.

The artwork in Nefertari's tomb is still bright and colorful.

An Italian explorer found the tomb of the Egyptian queen Nefertari in 1904 CE. It was in the Valley of the Queens. This is not far from the Valley of the Kings. The tomb is known for its detailed decorations.

Ancient Egyptians had respect for the dead. And they wanted a good **afterlife**. They were committed to building outstanding tombs to honor their dead.

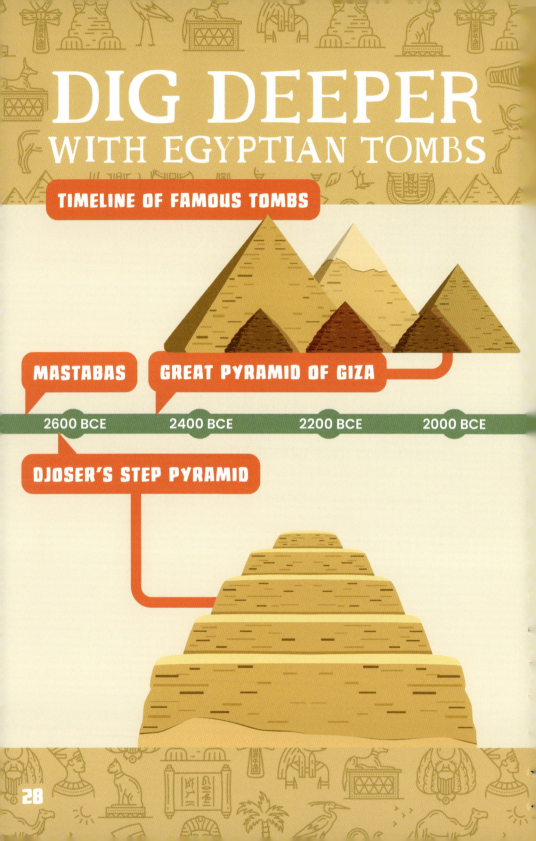

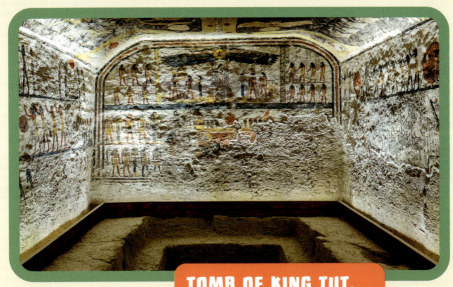

TOMB OF KING TUT, VALLEY OF THE KINGS

1800 BCE — 1600 BCE — 1400 BCE — 1200 BCE

TEMPLE OF HATSHEPSUT, NEAR VALLEY OF THE KINGS

TOMB OF RAMSES IX, VALLEY OF THE KINGS

MAKING CONNECTIONS

TEXT-TO-SELF

If you were pharaoh, which type of tomb would you have people build for you? Why?

TEXT-TO-TEXT

Have you read about the tombs of other ancient societies? How were they similar to and different from Egyptian tombs?

TEXT-TO-WORLD

What are some burial places near you? Do you think it is important to protect these places? Why or why not?

GLOSSARY

afterlife — life that exists after physical death.

archaeologist — a scientist who studies past human societies through the things left behind.

mummy — a dead body that is prepared so it doesn't break down like normal.

pharaoh — the highest ruler in ancient Egypt.

plaster — a paste that hardens to hold things together.

pyramid — a structure with a square base and four triangular sides that create a pointed top.

underworld — in some religions, a large place beneath the earth where dead people go.

INDEX

archaeologist, 4, 6–7, 21, 24

Great Pyramid of Giza, 12, 14, 28

King Tut, 21, 24, 29

mastaba, 8, 11–12, 25, 28

Nefertari, 27

Saqqara, 25

Snefru, 13–14

Step Pyramid, 12, 25, 28

Valley of the Kings, 6, 19, 21, 24, 27, 29

ONLINE RESOURCES
popbooksonline.com

Scan this code* and others like it while you read, or visit the website below to make this book pop!

popbooksonline.com/egyptian-tombs

*Scanning QR codes requires a web-enabled smart device with a QR code reader app and a camera.